Hindu
Priest

Rasamandala Das
Photographs by Chris Fairclough

W
FRANKLIN WATTS
LONDON•SYDNEY

First published in 2001 by
Franklin Watts
96 Leonard Street
London EC2A 4XD

Franklin Watts Australia
56 O'Riordan Street
Alexandria
NSW 2015

ISBN 0 7496 4063 4

Dewey Decimal Classification Number 294.5

A CIP catalogue record for this book is
available from the British Library

Series Editor: Ruth Nason
Design: Carole Binding

Reading Consultant: Lesley Clark, Reading
and Language Information Centre, University
of Reading

The Author and Publishers thank
Jai Krishna, his family and everyone at the
Bhaktivedanta Manor Temple for their kind
help in preparing this book.

Printed in Malaysia

Contents

Hello!

I am Jai Krishna. I am going to tell you about my life and work as a Hindu priest at a temple near London.

I will also tell you about my visits to India, the country where Hinduism started, long ago.

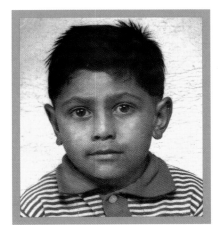

Before I was born my parents moved from India to Kenya. When I was 8 years old, we all moved to England.

Now I am married to Rukmini. We have two children. Our son, Ekachakra, is 8 years old and Varsha is 7.

A new day

Each day I get up very early – at 4 o'clock in the morning. I am not always happy to hear the alarm clock!

It is important for Hindus to be clean. I shower every morning. Then I put on my dhoti (robe) and chaddar (shawl). I also mark my forehead with a special clay from India. It is called tilak.

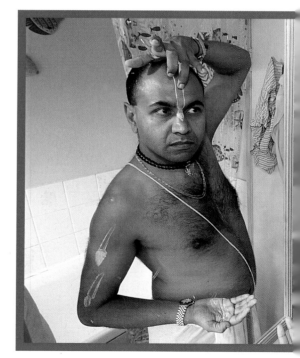

When I am dressed, I begin my morning prayers. I use a string of 108 beads to count the prayers I say.

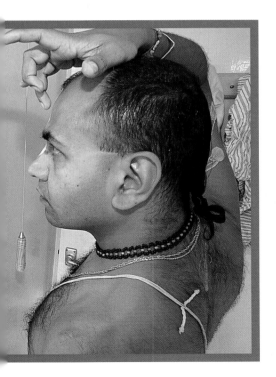

The temple

After my prayers I drive to the temple. Many Hindu temples in Britain look like ordinary buildings, but they always have an orange flag outside.

Hindus believe that the temple is God's home. So, out of respect, we take off our shoes before going in.

We believe that God appears in many different ways. These forms of God are called deities, and they have different names. There are statues of Rama and Krishna and other deities in the shrines at our temple.

A priest's job is to serve the deities. Early in the morning I bathe and dress them. At 8 o'clock I offer them their breakfast.

Arti

Arti is a ceremony to greet and worship the deities. At our temple, arti takes place seven times every day.

I blow a conch-shell loudly to tell everyone that the arti is starting. Then I offer a lamp to the deities, by moving it in circles in front of them. I also offer water, incense and a flower.

At the end of the ceremony, I fan the deities with a whisk.

Many worshippers come for the arti. Someone sings, and drums and cymbals keep the rhythm.

Then everyone joins in, singing, clapping and dancing.

Learning

Every morning, I study the Hindu holy books.

Then I have my breakfast and go to the temple school. I teach the children about the Hindu way of life.

I also teach them stories about God, who sometimes comes down to this world. We talk about Krishna and his girlfriend, Radha, and how they used to care for the cows.

We find out about Rama, too. In one shrine in our temple, the sacred statue or murti of Rama stands between his wife, Sita, and his brother, Lakshman. Hanuman, the monkey warrior, is in front of them.

Festivals

Festivals are busy times. Many people crowd into the temple for worship.

We put on dance shows and plays in our theatre. I make sure that everyone knows what to do. Here I am teaching Varsha a dance for the next festival – Krishna's birthday.

The biggest festival is Diwali – the festival of lights. Everyone offers lamps in front of the shrine. We remember how light drives away darkness and God destroys evil.

At Diwali we also celebrate how Rama killed the wicked king, Ravana. In our play, I was Ravana.

Special events

The temple is a place where Hindu people meet and celebrate special events like getting married.

At a wedding ceremony the bride and groom swop flower garlands. This shows their love for each other.

On these special days we have a sacred fire ceremony. Worshippers chant prayers and throw rice and barley into the flames. We believe that God eats what we offer in the fire.

Ekachakra wants to be a Hindu priest when he grows up. Here he is using a long wooden spoon to pour ghee (oil made from butter) onto the sacred fire.

Visiting India

Every year I go on pilgrimage to India. As I walk by the sacred river Yamuna, I remember that this is where Krishna lived 5,000 years ago.

His village is called Vrindavan and has thousands of temples. We stay in one that is made of marble.
In the gardens I teach students about the history of their religion.

Helping others

One of the jobs of a priest is to help other people. Every day I help to load the 'Food for All' van. It goes from our temple to London, where we feed more than 200 poor and homeless people. All the meals are vegetarian.

Caring for animals

At the temple we have a special farm without
any tractors. The bulls plough the land and
pull carts. The cows give milk for the temple.
Hinduism teaches us to be kind to animals.
The cows and bulls are never killed for eating.

Hinduism at home

Much Hindu worship and celebration takes place at home. Often I visit people's houses for a special event.

Many families ask me to perform a hair-cutting ceremony. This celebrates a boy's first hair-cut.

At our own home we have arti every evening. Like most Hindu families, we have a small shrine in the living room.

Here Varsha is fanning the murtis with the white whisk. Rukmini is singing, and Ekachakra is playing the drum.

After arti it's dinner time. Eating as a
family reminds us that we are trying to
serve God together. Before we eat, we offer
the meal to God by placing it in front of the
shrine. It is then called prasad – holy food.

At bedtime, I read the children stories about Rama, Krishna and their other heroes. Varsha falls asleep cuddling her favourite Krishna doll.

Then Rukmini and I have time to relax and talk about the day. At 10 o'clock we also go to bed. Tomorrow will be another busy day serving Krishna!

Glossary

arti

The main ceremony in a Hindu temple.

celebrate

To show that you are happy about something.

ceremony

Something we do on special occasions, usually in the same way every time.

chaddar

A cloth or shawl worn round the shoulders.

conch-shell

A large seashell used by Hindus in the arti ceremony.

deity

A being believed to have great power over people's lives; often a form of God.

dhoti

A robe worn by some men in India instead of trousers.

God

The most powerful being, who made everything; the greatest deity.

Hindu

A person who follows Hinduism.

Hinduism

The oldest religion in the world. It started more than 5,000 years

ago in India, and it is the main religion there today.

holy
Special. The word is used for something that people respect because it is connected with God.

incense
Sticks which are burned to make a nice smell.

murti
A sacred statue, usually of one of the Hindu deities.

offer
To give or show something to God, so that he can enjoy it.

pilgrimage
A journey or visit to a holy place.

priest
The man or woman who looks after the worship in the temple.

sacred
Another word for holy.

shrine
A holy place where people worship.

temple
A building where Hindus worship God.

vegetarian
With no meat in it; or a person who does not eat meat.

whisk
The white hair from the tail of an ox, used in the arti ceremony. In India a white whisk is a sign of a very special person, like a king.

Index